SHIPS AHOY!
Tugboats
by Kaitlyn Duling
BLASTOFF! 2 READERS
BLASTOFF! READERS, AN IMPRINT OF BELLWETHER MEDIA BY FLUTTERBEE

Blastoff! Readers are carefully developed by literacy experts to build reading stamina and move students toward fluency by combining standards-based content with developmentally appropriate text.

Level 1 provides the most support through repetition of high-frequency words, light text, predictable sentence patterns, and strong visual support.

Level 2 offers early readers a bit more challenge through varied sentences, increased text load, and text-supportive special features.

Level 3 advances early-fluent readers toward fluency through increased text load, less reliance on photos, advancing concepts, longer sentences, and more complex special features.

★ Blastoff! Universe

Reading Level

Grade
K

Grades
1–3

Grade
4

This edition first published in 2026 by Bellwether Media, Inc.

For information regarding permission, write to Bellwether Media, Inc., Attention: Permissions Department, 3500 American Blvd W, Suite 150, Bloomington, MN 55431.

Library of Congress Cataloging-in-Publication Data is available at www.loc.gov or upon request from the publisher.

ISBN: 9798893048032 (hardcover)
ISBN: 9798893049039 (ebook)

Editor: Kieran Downs Designer: Jennifer Bowyer

Printed in the United States of America, North Mankato, MN.

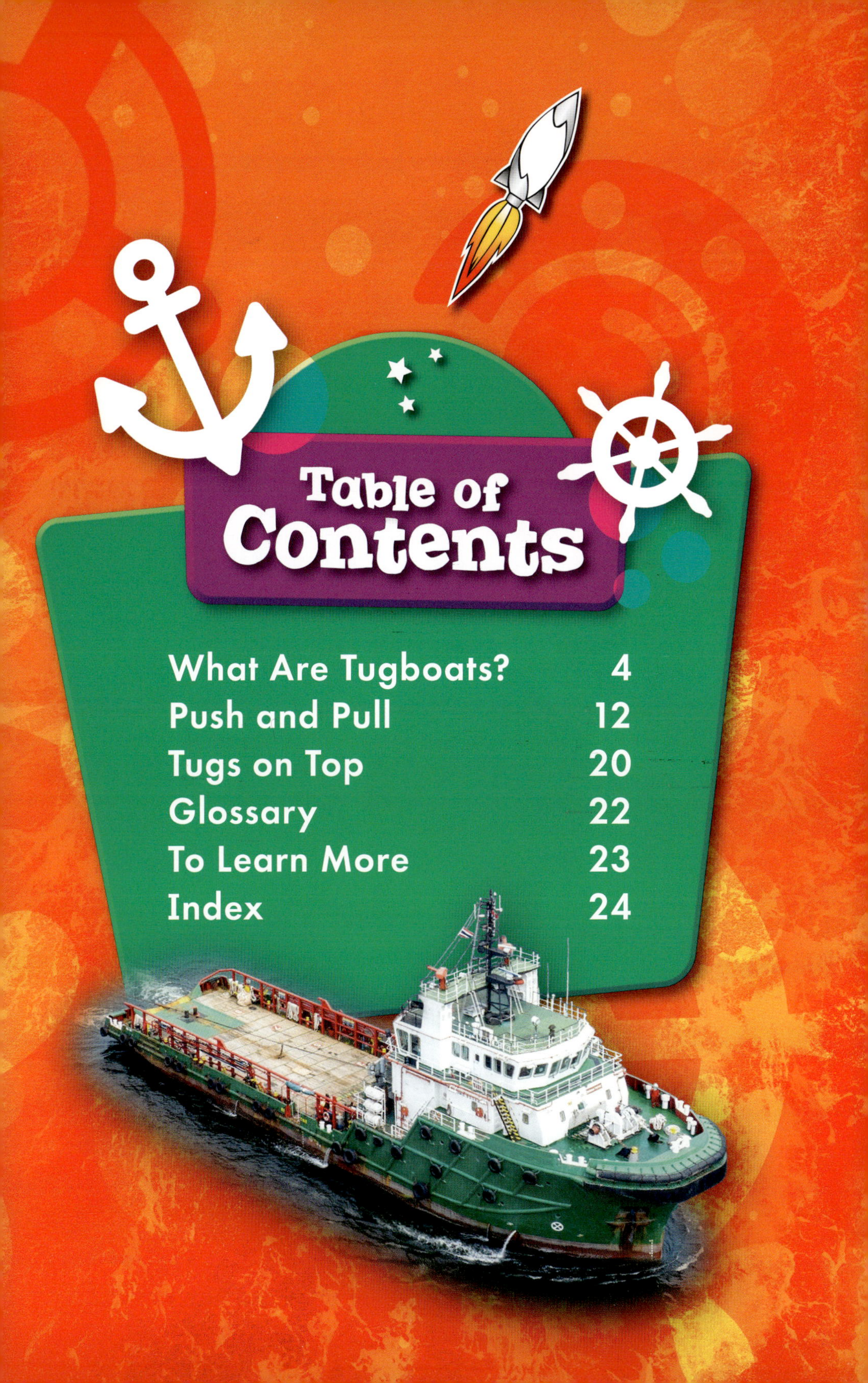

Table of Contents

What Are Tugboats?	4
Push and Pull	12
Tugs on Top	20
Glossary	22
To Learn More	23
Index	24

What Are Tugboats?

Tugboats are small ships that help move larger ships. They are sometimes called tugs.

Tugboats push and pull to move the larger ships.

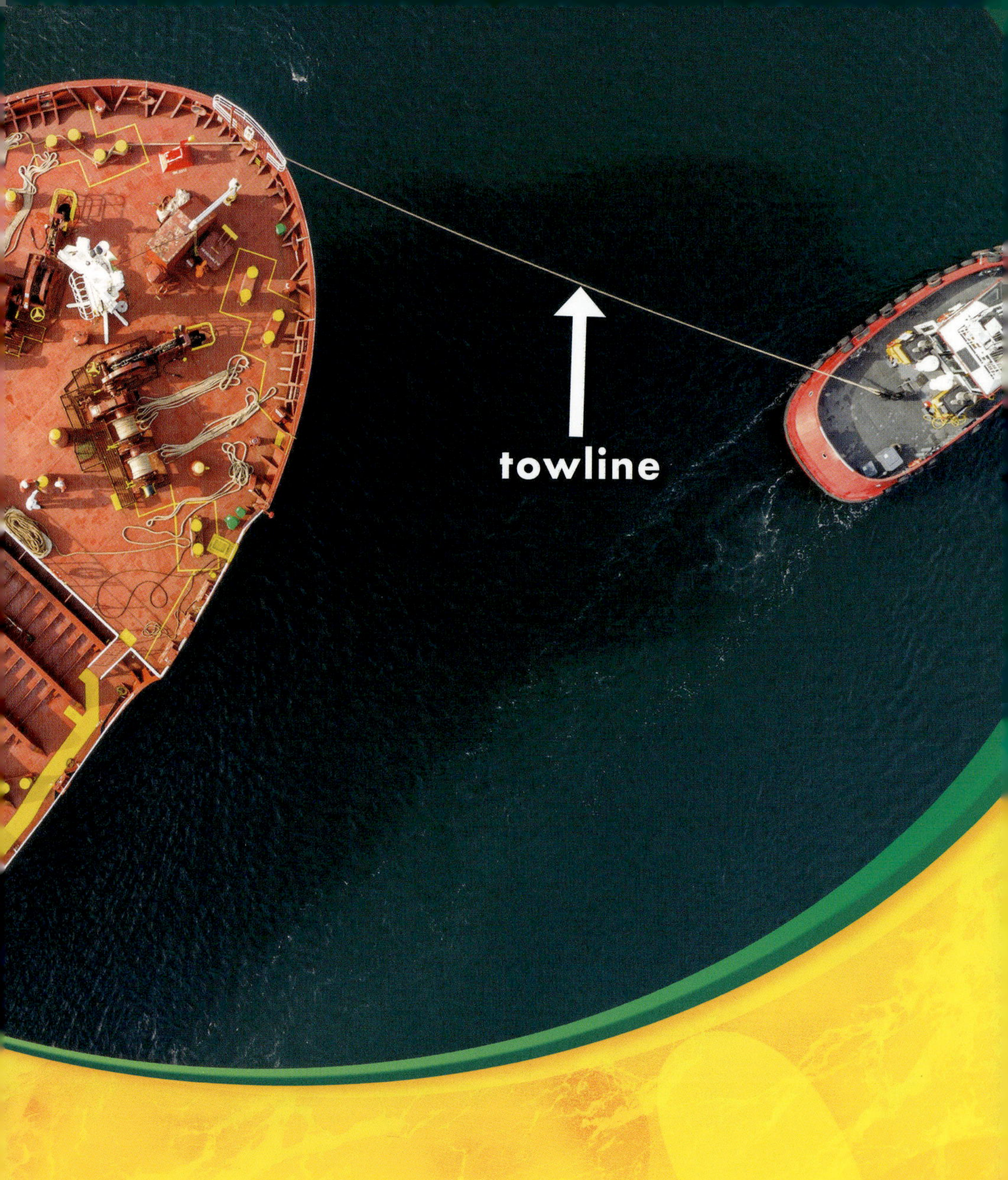

towline

Tugboats attach to ships with a **towline** to pull them.

When tugboats push, their **hull** is protected by **fenders**.

Tugboats are controlled from the pilothouse.

Engines are kept in the engine room. The engine powers the **propellers**. This helps tugs move.

pilothouse
engine

Types of Tugboats

river tugboat

harbor tugboat

ocean tugboat

River tugboats push **barges** on rivers. Harbor tugboats move easily in busy **ports**.

barge

Ocean tugboats have strong engines to move the largest ships at sea.

Push and Pull

Each tugboat carries just a few crew members. They work closely with people on ships and in ports.

Tugboats **signal** other ships using lights, whistles, and radios.

The captain turns a wheel to turn the tugboat. They can pull a lever to move the **rudders**.

The **mate** helps the captain.
They both work in the pilothouse.

Crew members attach the tugboat to bigger ships.

Tugboats sometimes work with other tugs. Many tugs can work together to move larger ships!

Connecting a Tugboat

1 The larger ship tells the tugboat where it needs to go.

2 The tugboat approaches the larger ship.

3 Crew members on the tugboat attach the towline to the larger ship.

4 The tugboat tells the larger ship that it is connected.

5 The tugboat pulls the larger ship.

Engineers work in the engine room.

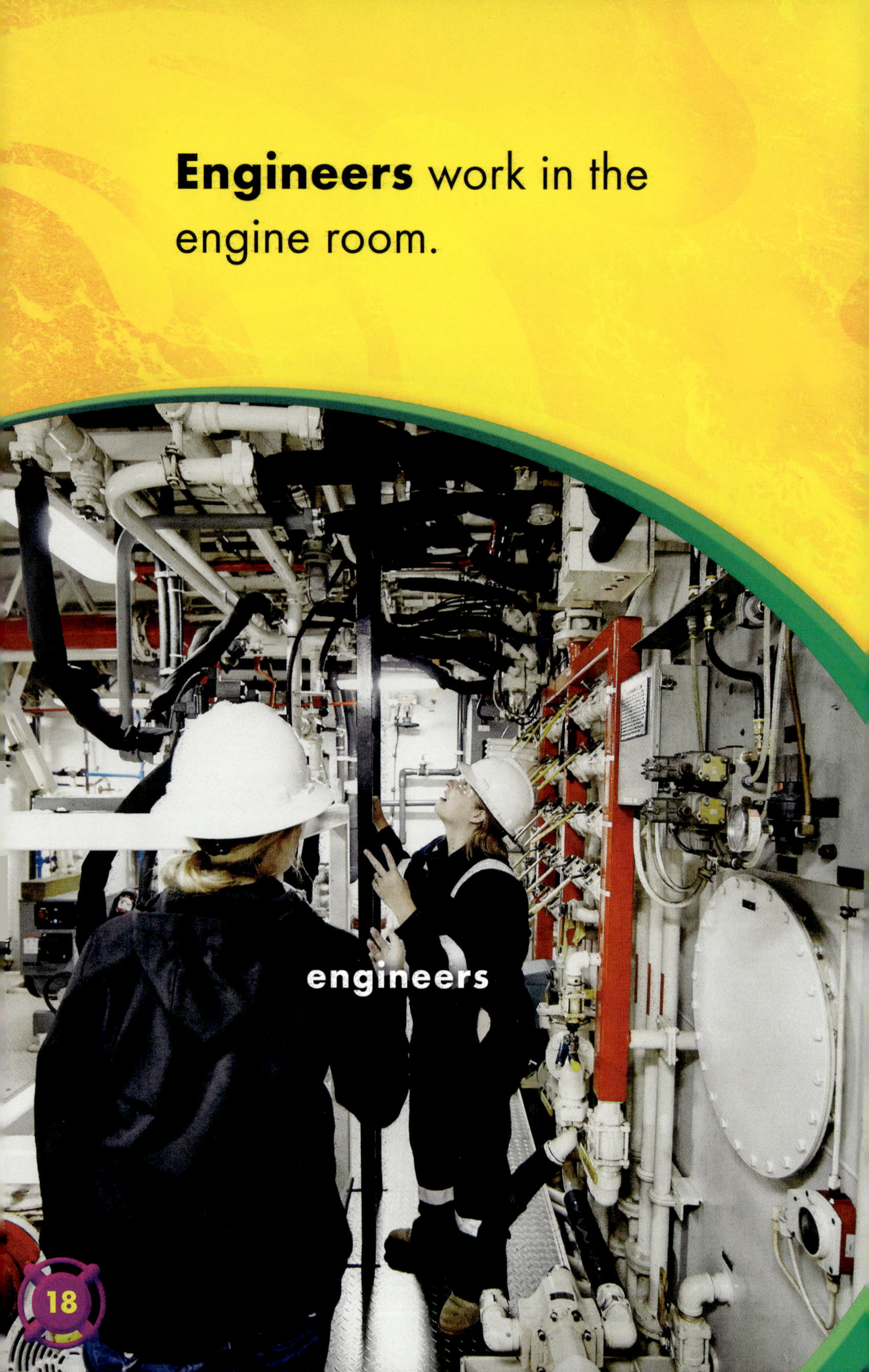

Most tugboats have two engines. These help tugs reach speeds of around 15 **knots** (17 miles or 27 kilometers per hour).

Tugs on Top

Tugboats help big ships move. They can also break up ice on water and fight fires.

Some tugboats help ships that are in trouble. Tugs are tiny heroes!

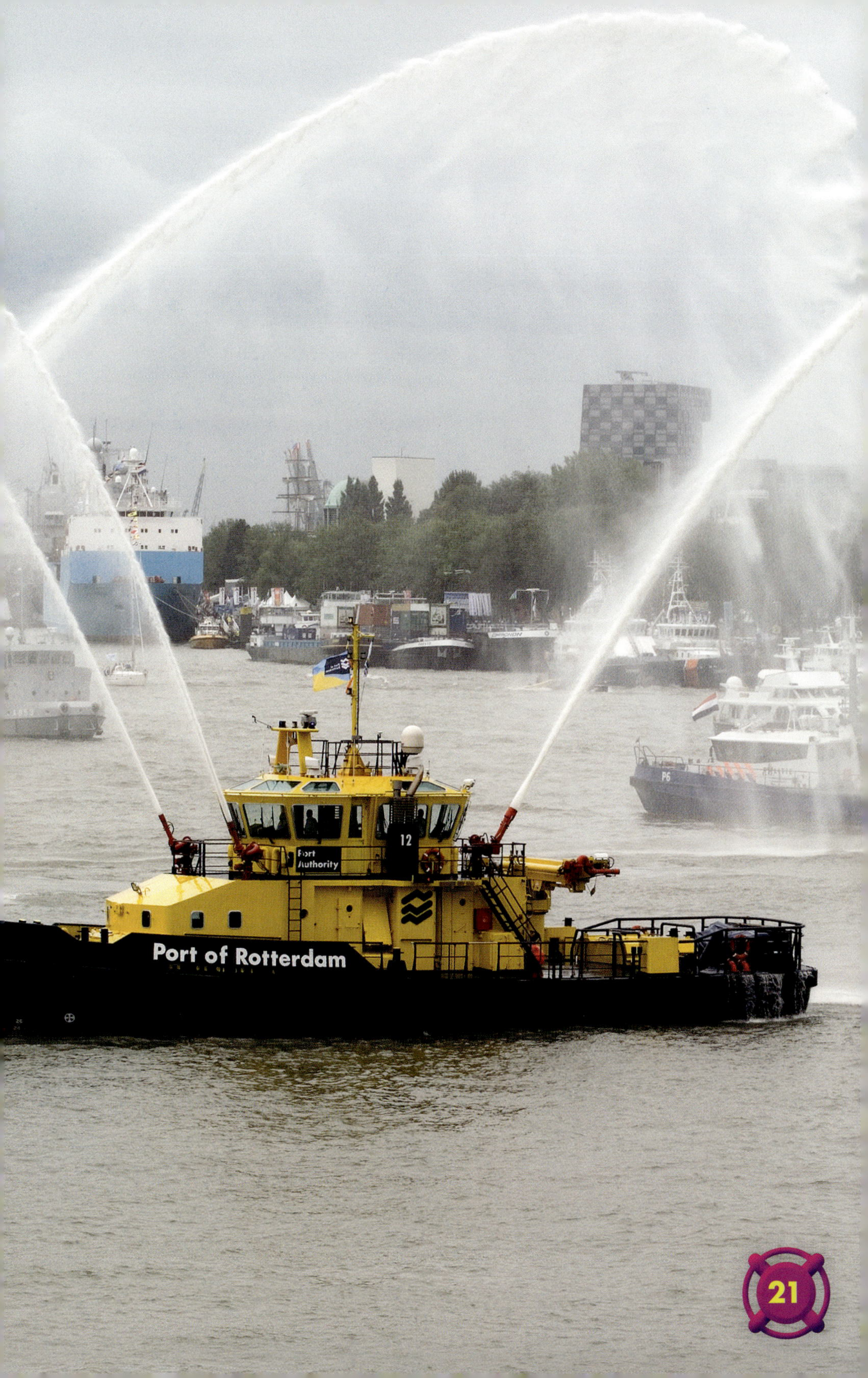
12
Port Authority
Port of Rotterdam
P6

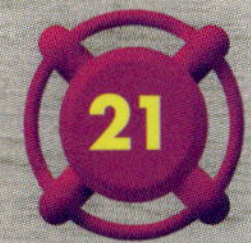

Glossary

barges—long, narrow, flat-bottomed boats

engineers—people who repair engines on a ship

engines—machines with moving parts that change power into motion

fenders—cushions or bumpers used to protect a ship from damage

hull—the main body of a ship

knots—units of measurement used to explain the speed of a ship

mate—an officer who helps direct the ship and keep the crew safe

ports—places where ships are loaded and unloaded

propellers—sets of spinning blades that help ships move

rudders—flat pieces used to turn

signal—to send a message without using words

towline—a rope or cable used to pull a ship

To Learn More

AT THE LIBRARY

Pang, Ursula. *Boats*. Buffalo, N.Y.: Powerkids Press, 2024.

Ritchie, Scot. *Tug: A Log Boom's Journey*. Toronto, Ontario: Groundwood Books, 2022.

Schwartz, Heather E. *Can Boats Fly? Questions and Answers about Water Vehicles*. North Mankato, Minn.: Capstone, 2025.

ON THE WEB

FACTSURFER

Factsurfer.com gives you a safe, fun way to find more information.

1. Go to www.factsurfer.com.
2. Enter "tugboats" into the search box and click .
3. Select your book cover to see a list of related content.

Index

captain, 14, 15
Carlo Magno, 13
crew, 12, 16
engineers, 18
engines, 7, 8, 9, 11, 18, 19
fenders, 7
hull, 7
mate, 15
pilothouse, 7, 8, 9, 15
propellers, 8
rudders, 14
speed, 19
towline, 6

The images in this book are reproduced through the courtesy of: FarisFitrianto, front cover; GreenOak, p. 3; Jake Warga/ Getty Images, pp. 4-5; Thanasis F, p. 5; Michael Dechev, pp. 6-7; Corepics VOF, pp. 7 (engine room), 9 (engine); Just dance, p. 7; Tawansak, p. 8; anucha sirivisansuwan/ Getty Images, pp. 8-9; Baloncici, p. 10 (river tugboat); Bildagentur Zoonar GmbH, p. 10 (harbor tugboat); mark_vyz, p. 10 (ocean tugboat); jrslompo, pp. 10-11; Monty Rakusen/ Getty Images, pp. 12-13, 14-15, 17 (1-4); Hannes Van Rijn/ Shipspotting.com, p. 13; Archive PL/ Alamy Stock Photo, p. 13 (inset); FLYTURK, p. 14; DigitalVues/ Alamy Stock Photo, p. 14 (rudders); bugto/ Getty Images, pp. 16-17; triple_v, p. 17 (5); Thomas Barwick/ Getty Images, pp. 18-19; Eli Wilson, p. 19; Marc Dufresne/ Getty Images, p. 20; Gaby Kooijman, pp. 20-21.